THE POCKET GUIDE TO

PREPPER KNOTS

A PRACTICAL RESOURCE TO KNOTS
THAT CAN HELP YOU SURVIVE

PATTY HAHNE

Skyhorse Publishing

Skyhorse Publishing books may be purchased in bulk at special discounts for sales promotion, corporate gifts, fund-raising, or educational purposes. Special editions can also be created to specifications. For details, contact the Special Sales Department, Skyhorse Publishing, 307 West 36th Street, 11th Floor, New York, NY 10018 or info@skyhorsepublishing.com.

Skyhorse® and Skyhorse Publishing® is a registered trademark of Skyhorse Publishing, Inc.®, a Delaware corporation.

Visit our website at www. skyhorsepublishing.com

10 9 8 7 6

Library of Congress Cataloging-in-Publication Data is available on file.

Cover design by Tom Lau
Cover image: iStockphoto

ISBN: 978-1-5107-1606-3
Ebook ISBN: 978-1-5107-1607-0

Printed in China

Contents

Disclaimer

The purpose of this book is to help teach people about several knots that preppers might find useful in both everyday life and in survival situations. It's the goal of the author to provide helpful information about the knots she thinks would be useful to preppers. While this book contains information about a number of knots, it's important to understand that it isn't all-inclusive, nor is it meant to be.

It's entirely possible that the author may not have mentioned certain knots you might need in an emergency situation. The author hopes this book will help you by teaching you how to tie some knots you might find useful, but *you alone are ultimately responsible for ensuring that you become proficient with any other knots you think your family may need to use in order to survive an emergency situation.*

The author has tried to provide the most accurate information she can in this book and she believes the information provided herein was correct at the time this book was written. She has tried to provide accurate instructions about the way *she ties the knots* described in this book but it may be possible for mistakes to exist in the way she ties them. There are often multiple methods of tying the same knot. Some may be more effective than others. The author makes no guarantee that the method she uses to tie knots is the most effective or correct.

The use of rope and/or knots can be inherently danger-ous, even life-threatening. It's possible for someone to be injured, or even killed, when using ropes and knots. As the person using and tying knots, *you alone bear the full burden and responsibility for the safety of people and/or property when making use of any instructions, photographs, commentary, or other material contained within this book, even if the information published in this book contains errors or incomplete information and/or instructions.*

Any trademarks mentioned in this book are included for editorial purposes only. These trademarks are the property of their respective owners.

The information contained in this book is intended for informational purposes only. The author claims no liability for the use or misuse of anything you might read in it.

Safety Warning

Keep in mind that the use of some of the knots written about in this book may pose safety hazards. Working with rope and/or knots can be inherently dangerous in some situations. One thing to always remember is that tying a knot in rope, string, fishing line, etc. will always weaken it to some degree. If any of these types of cordage break, it will often happen where the knot is tied unless the particular cordage has been damaged in another location. When choosing the type of rope and/or knot to use, you should keep in mind that a knot is usually the weakest link in a rope that is in good condition.

The author has tried to provide safety warnings where she feels it is appropriate, but ultimately it's *your responsibility* to determine if the use of any particular rope or knots require any special safety precautions. Be sure to always follow any applicable safety procedures and/or wear appropriate safety gear when using rope and tying knots. Additionally, the use of rope and some knots may pose a strangulation hazard. Even when all safety procedures are followed, rope can break and knots can fail.

Do not allow children or people who aren't mentally or physically capable of safely handling or using any items mentioned in this book access to them. If you choose to allow anyone to handle items that could be hazardous, you are doing so at your own risk.

An additional safety measure is to always double- and even triple-check the condition of the rope and that the knots are actually tied correctly. This is especially true if someone else has already tied a knot you will be relying on. Don't make the mistake of assuming they tied it correctly. In situations where personal injury and/or property damage could occur due to an incorrectly tied knot and/or damaged rope, it's always better to be safe and perform a thorough inspection.

About the Author

Patty Hahne is the author of preppersillustrated.com, an online magazine designed to help people with their emergency preparedness needs. She is also the author of *The Doomsday Prepping Crash Course: The Ultimate Prepper's Guide to Getting Prepared When You're on a Tight Budget.*

That book was based on two eBooks she had previously written titled, *Doomsday Prepping Crash Course: The Ultimate Prepper's Guide to Getting Prepared When You're on a Tight Budget* and *Build the Ideal Bug Out Bag: The Ultimate Guide to Preparing a 72 Hour Survival Kit for Surviving Comfortably.*

Her most recent book, *The Pocket Guide to Prepping Supplies: More than 200 Items You Can't be Without* was published in Spring 2016. All of the above mentioned titles are available on amazon.com.

Introduction

The use of rope and knots go hand and hand in the prepping world. Many preppers go to extreme lengths to stockpile items such as food, water, and medical supplies. Unfortunately, one thing they are often lacking is essential in emergency preparedness and it's stored right between their ears. This missing link is good old-fashioned knowledge.

It's not uncommon for people who are concerned about preparing for major catastrophes to stockpile rope, and it's important for them to take the time to learn about and become proficient in tying the various knots they might need in a survival scenario. Knowledge, when paired with training and practice, results in developing essential survival skills.

Rope is an important survival item but without the proper knowledge and experience in tying the correct knot for a particular task, it's just a piece of rope. It becomes a valuable survival tool when the user has acquired the necessary knowledge to select the appropriate knot for a particular situation and the skill to tie it proficiently.

Take a minute and think about that last paragraph. How many uses for rope can you think of that don't require one or more knots? Sure, you may be able to think of a few, but even if you can, there's probably a knot that can help you perform the task better and more safely.

After reading this book and practicing to become proficient with the knots you'll learn about in it, you will hopefully be even more prepared for whatever you might find yourself faced with in the future.

What This Book Is Not About

If you're looking for the most comprehensive encyclopedia on every type of knot in existence, this probably isn't the right book for you. On the other hand, if you would like to learn how to tie some very useful "multi-purpose" knots that can be used in a variety of situations, you're reading the right book!

Many other books have been written that contain instructions for tying more knots and that's fine, they definitely have their place. This book was written with the "less is more" philosophy in mind.

If you ever find yourself in a real-life survival situation, it's going to be stressful. When people are under stress, it can be difficult to think clearly. Some people may read a book that contains instructions on how to tie hundreds of knots and attempt to learn as many as they can. When the chips are down and you really need to remember the skills that will help you survive, the author would personally prefer to be *really proficient* in tying fewer knots that have *multiple uses* than feebly trying to remember how to tie one of hundreds she may have read about in a book.

Some people may choose to tie the knots discussed in this book when engaged in mountaineering but the author is not experienced in mountaineering and therefore will not recommend particular knots for that purpose.

Introduction to Various Types of Rope

If you are of the mindset that rope is just rope, you would be mistaken. There are many different types of rope to choose from when it comes to using it for prepping, survival, or practicing bushcraft skills. It's not uncommon to hear the word *cordage* used as a general term to describe items like rope, string, twine, or fishing line.

When it comes to tying knots, it doesn't matter how skilled you are if you are using the wrong type of rope for a particular situation. If you use the wrong type of rope, there's a very high likelihood that it will break or slip and the place it will usually fail is exactly where you tied the knot.

Additionally, factors such as rope that has been wet and left to mildew or left out in the elements and damaged by prolonged exposure to the sun may be unsafe to work with in critical applications. A good rule worth remembering is "when in doubt, throw it out." It's not worth risking safety or damage to property when it comes to tying knots with rope that is in poor condition.

Rope is manufactured in a variety of shapes, sizes, colors, and materials. Some rope is simply braided. Sometimes it has a braided cover with an inner core and sometimes it's braided and has a hollow core, meaning that it has a braided cover but no inner core. Other times, multiple strands of cordage are twisted together. There are so many variables that affect the quality and performance of rope that it would be impossible to list them all in one book.

Keeping in mind that the purpose of this book isn't to teach you what type of rope to use for a particular activity, suffice it to say that not all rope is created equal. For example, you may be able to purchase inexpensive rope at your local hardware store that looks somewhat similar to high-end climbing rope designed to protect you from life-threatening falls. Whatever you do, don't make the mistake of thinking cheap hardware store rope designed to look like climbing rope is appropriate for that particular activity. It's definitely not!

From a prepper's perspective, there are four primary types of cordage one might choose to stockpile:

550 Paracord: This particular type of rope is perhaps one of the most commonly used types of cordage in the prepping community. It's relatively thin and lightweight yet it has a very high strength-to-weight ratio. It's manufactured from nylon and was originally designed to serve as suspension lines between a parachute canopy and a parachute harness. It got its name because in order to meet military specifications, it needed to have a minimal tensile strength of 550 pounds.

One thing that's important to keep in mind is that it's possible to purchase products that are advertised as paracord that do not meet the specifications of having a 550 pound tensile strength. One helpful tip is to make sure that you are purchasing paracord that is labeled "MIL-C-5040H type III." This is the designation the United States military has given for the particular type of paracord they use.

It is typically around 4 mm in diameter. It has an outer woven sheath

Figure 1.

that typically encases seven inner core strands of cordage. Each of these seven core strands are typically made up of even more thinner strands that are twisted together. Figure 1 shows a photograph of 550 paracord that has a portion of the cover cut away revealing the inner twisted strands of cordage. Note that the paracord in this photo is included to give you a general idea of what paracord typically looks like. The paracord shown in this photo may not actually meet the MIL-C-5040H type III standard.

The main reason so many survivalists and preppers like 550 paracord is because of the unique way it is constructed. In an emergency, this particular type of rope can be cut and the inner strands can be removed to provide more useable cordage. Taking this a bit further, the strands that are removed can be untwisted, which provides even more thin cordage that can be used for things like snares or fishing line.

It's a very versatile type of cordage that is hugely popular in the prepping community. Not only is it versatile, it's relatively inexpensive, which means you can purchase quite a large quantity of it without having to dip into your kid's college fund.

Regardless of its advertised load rating of 550 pounds, *don't ever make the mistake of thinking that because you weigh less than 550 pounds that this type of cordage is safe for supporting your weight in a life or death situation.* Depending upon how much you weigh, it may be adequate for hanging a hammock between a couple of trees, but you should never put too much trust in it or use it in activities that could result in injury or property damage.

Climbing Rope: Keep in mind that climbing rope must be very high quality and have the specific characteristics for the type of job it will be doing. You'll most definitely pay a premium for real climbing rope. A hank of this type of rope in a length that would be appropriate for mountaineering activities such as climbing or rapelling can run $200 and up! If you intend to engage in any of these activities, make sure you are using the appropriate type of rope for the particular activity and that it isn't damaged in any way. Always remember that old rope may appear to be in good condition but, depending on how it has been used or stored, it may not be all it appears to be.

Marine Rope: This is rope specifically designed to be used on boats or in wet conditions. Rope that is not designed for wet conditions can mildew and rot, which will ultimately lead to it becoming weaker than its advertised breaking strength. One useful characteristic of this type of rope is that it will often float on water. A common type of marine rope is known as "double braid nylon rope" which has a braided outer hollow cover as well as a braided inner hollow core. It is often used on sailboats and one of the unique characteristics is that it can be spliced with the use of special tools. Figure 2 is a photograph of double braid nylon rope with an eye splice in one end. This particular rope is actually a dock line used for securing a boat to a dock.

Figure 2.

General Purpose Rope: This is the type of rope you typically find in the bargain bins at your big box home improvement stores. You can often pick up 50 to 100 feet of it for between five and ten dollars. This particular type of rope might be referred to as "junk" or "throwaway" rope. Despite the fact that it isn't designed to stand up to the rigors a high-quality mountaineering rope can withstand, there is definitely a place for it in prepping.

Keeping in mind that this type of cordage isn't designed to last for years or to support heavy loads, it's probably a good idea to have some around. Remember, this is low quality and inexpensive rope. Even if it says it has a particular tensile strength on the package, it would be wise to err on the side of caution and assume it will fail before that point. Tie a few knots in it and it will become even weaker.

Depending on the type of rope used, it may hold a knot differently. Some rope, such as polypropylene hollow braid rope, has a "plastic-like" feel. It's often used in wet environments since it tends to resist mildew and rot. The drawback to it is that it's slick and can be difficult to tie a knot in it that won't easily become untied.

The main thing to remember is you should practice tying knots with the type of rope you intend to use to see exactly what it feels like when you're tying knots in it. If you find it's quite difficult to work with or you find the knots you tie in it slip or don't want to stay tight, you might want to consider using a different type of rope.

Treating the Cut Ends of Rope

There will undoubtedly be occasions when you'll need to cut your cordage for one reason or another. With the exception of monofilament fishing line, the cut ends of a rope need to be treated in some way, otherwise it will quickly become an unraveled mess. Figure 3 shows an example of what the cut end of rope will do if it isn't treated properly.

There are four commonly used methods of dealing with the cut ends of rope to prevent unraveling:

Figure 3.

I. The first method is using heat to melt the loose ends into one solid mass. This method is commonly used for rope such as 550 paracord. It should be noted that this method won't work with rope constructed from fibers that don't actually melt when heat is applied to them. For example, natural fiber rope will just burn when heat is applied to it. This can be accomplished by cutting the rope with a "hot knife" or melting the end with a flame from a match or lighter. If you choose to use this method, there are some very important things to remember. *When you melt plastic, it will emit some nasty fumes that are hazardous to your health. Only do this in a well ventilated area and DO NOT breathe any of these fumes. You'll be using a hot knife or open flame so never melt the ends of rope around combustible materials. Lastly, melted rope is HOT AND STICKY! It may*

Figure 4.

even catch on fire and drip molten and/or flaming plastic-like drops. This melted material will stick to your flesh and cause severe burns. It may even start a fire if it lands on something combustible. Figure 4 is a photo of rope that has had the cut end melted to prevent fraying.

2. The second method is to "whip" the ends with "whipping twine." This method is commonly used to bind the ends of natural fiber rope or rope that is constructed from twisted strands. It's also quite common when using rope for boating to have the ends whipped. Whipping the end of a rope basically means you wrap whipping twine in tight concentric coils around the loose fibers at the end. There is a special technique that is often used when whipping rope where the loose ends of the whipping twine actually get pulled under the coils. Figure 5 shows a different whipping technique and the end of the rope after being melted.

Figure 5.

3. The third method is to wrap the loose ends tightly with some kind of tape. Electrical tape might work well because it can be wrapped very tightly. The disadvantage of this method is the tape may degrade and need to be replaced.

4. The fourth is to coat the cut ends with a product such as Whip-End Dip®. This is a water-based liquid vinyl product. When dry, this product produces a coating around the end of the rope designed to prevent the ends from fraying.

The type and quality of rope you're working with will dictate how much care should be taken when treating the cut ends. For example, some people who are working with rope that has an inner core will tape the end of the rope tightly, cut near the tape, melt the loose fibers, and finish by whipping the end.

The method you decide to use will be entirely up to you. The main thing to remember is when you cut a rope, you should always treat the cut ends using the appropriate method for the type of rope you are working with.

There's often an exception to these types of rules and this one is no different. If time is of the essence, you may choose to simply tie a knot in the end of the rope to keep it from unraveling. This isn't the ideal method but it might work in a pinch.

Making Use of Scavenged Rope

In a perfect world, we would all only use new rope or at least rope that is in very good condition. The reality of finding yourself suddenly placed in a survival situation could mean you may have to resort to scavenging for cordage. There are plenty of uses for rope you might be able to collect but you don't really know anything about scavenged rope.

You don't know the rated load capacity, how old it is, or how it has been stored. With this in mind, exercise extreme caution when using scavenged rope. It may be fine for your intended purposes or it may break easily. You'll have to assess the particular situation and decide for yourself if you feel like it is safe to use rope you have been able to collect.

Basic Knot-Tying Terminology

Now, let's take a moment and discuss the terms commonly used when tying knots and working with rope. If you familiarize yourself with these terms, it will make the process of learning to tie knots much easier. Figure 6 is a photo of a piece of rope with numbers that correspond to some of the terms described in this chapter.

Figure 6.

1. **Working End:** Also known as the "tag end." When you're talking about knots with fishermen, they'll most

likely use the term *tag end*. This is the end of the rope you are working with. In the case of tying a knot, it's the end you are actually tying the knot in. For example, if you are tying a fishing lure onto your line, the end you hold in your hand to tie the lure onto would be the working end.

2. **Standing End:** The opposite end of the rope that you tie a knot in. For example, if you use a knot to attach a rope to a log you intend to pull out of the woods for firewood, the end you are actually pulling on would be the standing end.

3. **Standing Part:** This is the section of rope between the working end and the standing end.

4. **Bight:** When you take a section of rope and form a bend that looks like the letter "u," you are creating a bight.

5. **Loop:** When you form a bight and then put one twist in it so that the working end and standing part cross, you have created a loop.

6. **Overhand Loop:** When you form a bight and then put one twist in it so that the working end is on top of the standing part, you have created an overhand loop.

7. **Underhand Loop:** When you form a bight and then put one twist in it so that the working end is under the standing part, you have created an underhand loop.

8. Elbow: If you form a bight and then put two twists in it, you have created an elbow.

Single Turn: If you pass the working end around something, you have made a single turn. For example, you create a single turn when you wrap a rope around a tree to tie a knot. Figure 7 illustrates what a single turn looks like.

Figure 7.

Round Turn: If you pass the working end around something to form a complete circle, you have made a round turn. For example, you create a round turn when you wrap a rope around a tree twice to tie a knot. For an example of what a round turn looks like, see figure 8.

Figure 8.

Hitch: This type of knot is generally used to attach a rope to something.

Hank: A term used to describe a length of rope.

Line: A term that originated from the sailing world that is often used to describe a length of cordage. This term is sometimes used throughout this book and is synonymous with the term *rope*.

Dressing: Before you pull a knot tight, there is an important step in the knot-tying process that is often called "dressing." This simply means that you take the time to look closely at the way the individual elements of the knot are laying and, if necessary, rearrange them. By making sure they are laying properly *before you pull the knot tight,* you're much more likely to end up with a correctly tied knot.

It's entirely possible, and not uncommon, for a person to follow all the steps necessary to tie a particular knot only to end up with one that isn't properly tied because they didn't take the time to dress it before pulling it tight.

It's important that you tie neat and tidy knots because if you don't, they may not perform the way they are intended to. *If the parts of the rope that make up the knot aren't lying properly before you tighten the knot, it may become untied when it is shaken or even slip and become untied under tension.*

Tightening: While it may not seem like this is worth mentioning, it's important for you to understand that when tying some knots, you need to dress the knot and tighten it during the actual process of tying it. If you just go through the motions and then pull on the rope, you're likely to end up with a jumbled mess that doesn't look anything like the knot you intended to tie.

Some knots will tighten upon themselves when a load is applied while others need to be properly tightened before putting any weight on the rope. It's a good practice to get into the habit of inspecting your knot closely while you're dressing it and tighten it before you put any weight on the standing part or standing end of the rope.

Stopper: This is a type of knot tied for the purpose of preventing rope from slipping through a knot or a hole such as a grommet in a tarp or rainfly on a tent. Many people tie a

Figure 9.

stopper knot in the working end of a rope as a precautionary measure after completing the primary knot. Figure 9 shows a clove hitch that has been tied around a branch. To help prevent slipping, an overhand knot has been tied as a stopper in the remaining length of the working end.

Critical Application: You'll see this term used in this book when referring to applications for various knots that pose a risk to personal safety or if there is a possibility of property damage when using particular knots. *It is the responsibility of the person using rope and/or tying knots to determine if the situation should be considered a critical application.*

Non-Critical Application: A term used throughout this book when referring to situations when you'll be using light-duty rope or string for situations when the failure of cordage or a knot won't pose a risk to personal safety or the possibility of property damage. *It is the responsibility of the person using rope and/or tying knots to determine if the situation should be considered a non-critical application.*

When a Knot is *NOT* a Knot

It's pretty easy to spot someone who doesn't know how to tie a proper knot. You've probably seen someone tie knot on top of knot thinking they are actually making it stronger. Maybe you've even been guilty of this a time or two and that's OK. The fact that you're taking the time to read this book means you realize there is a huge difference between properly tying a knot and merely making a jumbled mess of a piece of rope. In figure 10, you see an example of this.

Figure 10.

Tying the same knot on top of itself over and over doesn't necessarily make it better or stronger. A properly tied knot is simple and elegant. It performs its job easily and is often easy to untie.

You wouldn't use a spoon to cut a steak because you know it's not the right tool for the job. Keep this analogy in mind when you are deciding which knot to use for the job you want it to do. Every time you tie a knot, take a second and ask yourself what you are trying to accomplish by tying it in the first place. This will help you decide what knot is most appropriate for the particular application.

The Most Important Step in Learning to Tie Knots

Before moving on, you should know that the following knots are a compilation of knots that could be useful in prepping and survival situations. They were invented long before anyone ever used the term *prepper*. Nevertheless, for the purpose of this book, they are referred to as prepper knots. We will first cover some very basic knots to get your feet wet, so to speak, and then move on to more advanced knots as you gain experience. This seems like a good time to bring up one of the most important topics in this book: **When it comes to learning how to tie knots, nothing is more important than practice!**

Think of the last time you tied your shoelaces. Did you go to your bookshelf and pull out your trusty copy of *The Field Guide to Tying Your Shoelaces*? Of course not, because you've tied your laces so many times that it has become second nature to you. You've created what is referred to as "muscle memory." When you practice tying a knot enough times, you won't even have to think about the steps involved in tying it. You'll just do it, as if you always knew how. This should be your goal as you progress through this book.

How to Get the Most Out of This Book

In order to get the most out of this book, it really shouldn't be read cover to cover like you might read a novel. A better strategy would be to have some good quality rope handy and as you read about each knot, take the time to actually follow the instructions and learn how to tie the knots yourself.

Reading from cover to cover will familiarize yourself with the information this book contains but you won't ever become proficient at tying the knots described using this strategy. Remember, your ultimate goal should be to become so proficient at tying the knots in this book that you can tie them as easily as you tie your shoelaces.

Don't forget that when the chips are down and you're in "survival mode," you'll need to rely on the numerous hours you spent practicing to develop your knot-tying skills. You should be able to grab a piece of rope, and without thinking, know exactly what knot will be most appropriate for the task at hand and quickly tie it without having to pick this book up or struggle to try and remember how it is supposed to be tied. *In a real emergency, your life could actually depend on it!*

Something to Consider Before You Tie Any Knot

Regardless of what type of knot you tie, it's important for you to understand that it is friction that holds it in place. Without adequate friction, the cordage used to tie the knot may slip and the knot can become untied. This is most commonly seen with low-friction cordage such as monofilament fishing line and rope that has a plastic-like feel to it. Fishermen know all too well that if you don't use the proper type of knot when tying a hook or lure onto monofilament line, the line can actually slide through the knot and the hook will come off when put under the stress of trying to reel in a fish.

There are so many reasons you might want to tie a knot that it would be impossible to even attempt to name them all. With this in mind, there is a very important factor to consider when you are choosing the particular knot to tie. Each time you tie a knot, think about whether you'll ever need to untie it.

Some knots can be extremely difficult, if not impossible, to untie after a considerable amount of tension has been applied to the rope. Other knots, by the very nature in which they are used, cannot be untied at all. One example of this would be knots that are tied in small diameter fishing line or string.

If you understand the characteristics of various knots when they are tied in the many different types of rope, twine, string, or fishing line, you'll know whether it will be difficult to untie them should you ever need or want to. This will help you in deciding which knots to use and whether you want to tie knots that tend to be difficult to untie in your "good rope."

Always remember that cordage is a very important commodity in a survival situation, which means it should be treated with the utmost care. If you know a knot is going to be very difficult to untie and you aren't tying it for use in a critical application, you may want to consider using inexpensive rope that you can just cut if you aren't able to untie a particular knot.

During everyday life events, you may not care if you won't be able to untie a knot that you tie in the rope you are using. After all, you can always just cut the rope at the knot or buy another one, but when rope is in short supply, it would be prudent to remember that you'll most likely want to untie the knots you are tying so you can use the rope multiple times.

While on the subject of untying knots, it's important to understand the characteristics of the rope you are using.

Depending on factors like the material the rope is made from and its thickness, you'll discover that some types of rope create quite a bit of friction when a knot is tied in them. Remember, it's this friction that can make untying a knot very difficult.

Other types of cordage are slick and don't hold some knots very well at all. An example of this would be monofilament fishing line or rope that feels like slick plastic. A knot that might hold just fine with thicker rope can often slip and untie itself under tension when using monofilament. The number of inexperienced anglers who have tied a hook or lure onto their fishing line, only to watch the knot become untied when they hook a fish, would be way too high to count. Luckily for you, this book contains instructions for tying several good knots that aren't typically prone to slipping.

Considering that certain knots can slip when tension is applied, some people choose to tie stopper knots in the leftover length of the working ends of rope as an added precaution. The reason for doing this is that if the rope slips and the knot begins to become untied, the stopper knot may help to prevent it from slipping enough that it becomes completely untied.

You should know that it isn't usually advisable to trim the working ends off close to the knot. Doing so might make the knot look a bit tidier but it could increase the likelihood that the knot could slip and become untied. It isn't uncommon for a knot to slip a little bit before it really tightens down after tension is applied. For this reason, you might want to consider keeping your working ends a little long instead of trimming them close to the knot. Figure 11 shows a square knot that has the working ends cut off too close to the knot.

Figure 11.

In summary, know your rope, tie neat and tidy knots, and consider whether you'll ever want to be able to untie the knot you're tying, and if so, choose a knot that has characteristics that make it easy to untie.

Some Knot-Tying Pitfalls

There's no question that being proficient in tying the most suitable knot for a particular application is an important skill to have. Just as important is understanding that even properly tied knots in high-quality rope can sometimes fail.

You've undoubtedly heard the expression, "the weakest link." This actually refers to a chain, and if one link in the chain is weak or damaged, this is where the chain is most likely to break when under tension.

Unfortunately, *a knot is usually the weakest link in a length of rope*. While tying knots is necessary when working with rope, it's important to understand that any knot you tie will lower the rated tensile strength of the rope you are using.

It's beyond the scope of this book to provide exact figures in terms of how much each specific knot will decrease the tensile strength of different types of rope. There are just too many variables that come into play. If you would like specific data on this matter, you should contact the manufacturer of the rope you are using.

The important takeaway here is if you tie a knot in a rope that has no flaws and is in good condition, if it's going to break, it may break where the knot was tied. Why is this important, you might ask? For the sake of simplicity, let's assume you're using some heavy-duty string that has an advertised tensile strength of 100 lbs. If you tie a knot in a piece of this particular cordage that is known to weaken the tensile strength by 30 percent, theoretically that string should now only be capable of holding 70 lbs. before it might break. The bottom line is you should always remember that the knot is usually the weakest link in rope.

Another thing that is very important to understand is when knots are used incorrectly they may fail. Two common ways knots are prone to failing are "capsizing" and "slipping."

Capsizing may occur when a load is placed on a knot that is only intended to have a load applied in a certain direction. When a knot capsizes, the orientation of the rope is altered which results in the individual parts of the knot ending up in the incorrect position. This usually reduces the overall effectiveness of the knot, which may result in it slipping and becoming untied.

When you are tying a knot, think of each step as if you are putting a puzzle together. The pieces need to be put in the correct places to complete the puzzle. A knot is very similar. If the parts of the knot aren't in the correct position or orientation, it isn't tied properly and it could fail.

Slipping can result when a knot capsizes but it doesn't necessarily have to capsize in order for it to slip. Remember, knots depend on friction to do their job. Without enough friction, slipping can easily occur.

Imagine you are trying to pull a log to your campsite that you found in the forest. You tie what you think is a good knot around the log and you start dragging it along the forest floor. It's raining outside so your rope is wet and a bit slippery. As you pull on the rope, there isn't enough friction between the parts of the knot so the working end starts to slip through the knot. If you continue pulling, it's possible for the working end to slip enough that the entire knot will become untied.

Instructions for Tying Prepper Knots

Keep in mind that many knots are known by different names. Factors such as the part of the world you live in, or the application the knot is being used in, contribute to the same knot having multiple names. The author has tried to make a note if she is aware of alternate names of the knots she is describing.

If someone else happens to use a different name for the particular knots described in this book, that's just fine. The important thing is for you to understand what the intended purpose of the knots are and that you become proficient at tying them.

For your information, most of the rope used in the photographs included in this book is 3/8 inch double braid marine rope. It was chosen for illustration purposes because it is quite soft and pliable which makes illustrating the different steps in the knot-tying process easier.

When it's necessary to use two lengths of rope for a photograph, one rope will usually be red and the other will usually be dark blue. This is done for no other reason than these were the colors that were locally available to the author and they contrast nicely against each other for illustration purposes.

In some cases, blue and orange 550 paracord is used, particularly for illustrating the steps necessary for tying fishing knots. As you'll read later in this book, it would be next to impossible to provide helpful photographs if regular fishing line was used.

Note: *One thing that is very important to understand is that for the sake of showing what the finished knots should look like before you tighten them, in some cases the knots in the photographs that are illustrating the final step won't be completely tightened. This was done intentionally because it can sometimes be difficult to see what the knot should actually look like after it has been tightened.* ***When you tie knots that you plan on using for real-life practical applications, you should tighten the knots before using them.***

Overhand Knot

The most basic of knots is the common overhand knot. This is probably the one knot that nearly everyone inherently knows how to tie. It can be used as a stopper knot but many other knots are tied by first tying an overhand knot. For example, when you tie an overhand knot around an object such as a tree, pole, or grommet, it is called a "half hitch."

As you continue reading through this book, you will see that tying an overhand knot is often a step used in tying more complex knots.

Pros: This knot is extremely easy to tie.

Cons: Depending on the type of rope this knot is tied in, if it is put under a heavy load, it can be very difficult to untie. This is often the case when it is tied in very thin cordage.

How to tie it:

1. Form an overhand loop as illustrated in figure 12a.

Figure 12a.

2. Thread the working end up through from underneath the loop as illustrated in figure 12b.

Figure 12b.

3. Pull on the working end and the standing part to tighten the knot as illustrated in figure 12c.

Figure 12c.

Possible Uses:

1. Some knots may have a tendency to slip when a load is applied to them. Putting an overhand knot in the end of a rope can help to prevent a knot from coming untied when there is weight or tension applied to it—hence the reason it's often referred to as a "stopper knot."

2. If you have a rope that you are trying to hold onto while tension is applied to it, tying overhand knots in the end you're holding may help prevent the rope from sliding through your hand.

3. If you're hanging a tarp to set up a rain shelter, an overhand knot tied in the end of the rope can prevent the rope from sliding through the grommet on the tarp. Simply feed the standing end of the rope through the grommet and the overhand knot will stop the rope from slipping through the hole when you attach the working end to a tree, rock, or stake. That is, of course, if the rope is of large enough diameter that the knot won't just slip through the hole you threaded it through.

Figure 8 Knot

This is another stopper knot that is a slight variation of the overhand knot. It's also a building block for some other commonly used knots.

Pros: It's very easy to tie and often easier to untie than a simple overhand knot. The knot also has more bulk than the simpler overhand knot.

Cons: Depending on the type of cordage this knot is tied in, if the rope is put under a load, it can be difficult to untie.

How to tie it:

1. Form an overhand loop as illustrated in figure 13a.

Figure 13a.

2. Pass the working end under then around the standing part as illustrated in figure 13b.

Figure 13b.

3. Thread the working end down through the loop as illustrated in figure 13c.

Figure 13c.

4. Pull the knot tight. The finished knot will look similar to the number 8 as illustrated in figure 13d.

Figure 13d.

Possible Uses:

1. As mentioned, this is also a stopper knot and one reason for choosing a figure 8 knot over an overhand knot is that it provides a slightly larger stopper. This can be handy in situations where a simple overhand knot might slip though a grommet due to its size. Tying a figure 8 knot makes the stopper just a bit larger, which could prevent the knot from sliding through the hole it's threaded into.

2. This knot is also commonly used as a foundation for more complex knots used in mountaineering.

Figure 8 Loop

If you ever need to tie a relatively secure loop in your rope, you may want to consider using this knot. This knot is commonly used in mountaineering.

Pros: It's quite easy to tie, even in the middle of a length of rope, assuming that the rope isn't under tension.

Cons: Depending on the particular rope you are using, it might be difficult to untie this knot after a considerable amount of tension has been applied to the rope.

How to tie it:

1. Form a bight where you want to tie the figure 8 loop as illustrated in figure 14a.

Figure 14a.

2. Create an underhand loop with the bight as illustrated in figure 14b.

Figure 14b.

3. Pass the "u" in the bight over and around the standing part and working end as illustrated in figure 14c.

Figure 14c.

4. Thread the "u" in the bight up through the loop as illustrated in figure 14d.

Figure 14d.

5. Dress the knot by flipping down the part of the knot nearest to the loop, pull it tight, and you have tied a figure 8 loop. Your finished knot should look like the one seen in figure 14e.

Figure 14e.

Possible Uses:

1. The figure 8 loop can be used for attaching something to the working end or even a section along the standing part of a rope.

2. You can also use this knot to create a loop on the standing part that another rope can be tied into. This could come in handy for a variety of applications, such as securing a load to a trailer or even a boat.

Figure 8 Follow-Through Knot

When tying a rope around something with a figure 8 loop, you'll need to use a variation known as the "figure 8 follow-through knot." This one is tricky and it's easy to get confused while tying it. Pay very close attention to every step of the process to make sure you have each part of the knot in its proper place.

Pros: Many people trust and rely on this knot for critical applications when they want a more robust knot than a simple bowline.

Cons: This variation of the simple figure 8 loop takes more time to tie than a simpler knot like the bowline. Additionally, special attention should be taken to make sure this knot is properly dressed and tied for use in critical applications.

Note: For illustration purposes only, the following photographs show this knot being tied into a simple swivel snap. Please note that this type of snap *should never be used for critical applications* as it could break under tension.

How to tie it:

1. Tie a standard figure 8 knot in the working end. Make sure to leave enough extra rope on this end to complete the "follow through" portion of this knot. With enough practice, you'll get a feel for how much extra rope is actually needed.

2. Pass the working end through or around the object you want the loop to encompass as illustrated in figure 15a.

Figure 15a.

3. Add a little slack to the figure 8 knot you tied in step 1 to enlarge it slightly. This will make completing the remaining steps easier.

4. Thread the working end back through your original figure 8 knot taking care to make sure you retrace the

Figure 15b.

entire figure 8 precisely. Figure 15b illustrates the work-ing end that has been threaded back through the figure 8 knot.

5. To dress the knot, flip the top strand of the rope that is nearest to the standing part down so that the knot is symmetrical when inspecting it from both ends of the "8" and both sides of the knot. Figure 15c shows the top strand flipped down. Note the difference between how the knot looks in figure 15b and 15c. In figure 15c, the knot is nice and symmetrical.

Figure 15c.

6. Pull the knot tight and you have completed a figure 8 follow-through knot.

Optional Step: As an added measure of safety and security, many people tie a backup knot onto the standing part with the left over portion of the working end.

How to tie it:

1. Hold the standing part and your working end above the knot.

2. Cross the working end over the standing part as illustrated in figure 16a.

Figure 16a.

3. Wrap the working end behind and around to the front. You'll see that you've created a wrap around the standing part and the place where the wrap is now laying looks like the letter "x" as illustrated in figure 16b.

Figure 16b.

4. Make another wrap, keeping this one between the "x" and
the figure 8 follow-through knot as illustrated in figure
16c.

Figure 16c.

5. Thread the working end through both wraps as illustrated in figure 16d. You'll actually be threading it under
the "x" and away from the figure 8 follow-through knot.

Figure 16d.

6. Pull on the working end to tighten the backup knot. If you've tied it correctly, it should look like an "x" on one side and an "=" on the other. Figure 16e shows the way the entire figure 8 follow-through knot with a backup knot should look.

Figure 16e.

Note: This is a complex knot that is often used in critical applications. *After tying it, you should double- and triple-check to make sure it is tied correctly.* It's even a good practice to have someone else double-check to make sure the knot looks to be correctly tied.

Some people determine if their knot is tied correctly by getting into the habit of looking at the knot and making sure they have five pairs of two ropes followed by a backup knot. Remembering that the backup knot looks like the multiplication sign on one side and the equal sign on the other, you may want to use a mnemonic phrase such as 5 x 2 = 10. Five pairs, multiplied by two ropes in each pair, equals ten strands of rope. This is illustrated in Figure 17. If you flip the

Figure 17.

knot over, it should pass this inspection just like it did on the other side.

Possible Uses:

1. As mentioned before, this knot is commonly used in mountaineering. If you choose to use it for this purpose, you should first get training from a qualified instructor.

2. It can be used for similar purposes that the bowline is used for but it's considered to be a more secure knot by many people. For example, serious mountaineers would never tie into their harness using a simple bowline.

Square Knot

This is a commonly used knot for binding a bundle of objects together. Other than the basic overhand knot, the square knot is probably the most commonly known knot in existence. Depending upon what part of the world you live in, they may call this particular knot a "reef knot." Regardless of what name it is known by, it's the same knot.

While it may be a commonly known knot, *it should be used with great caution.* Many people are tempted to use this particular knot to tie two lengths of rope together to make one longer rope. This is NOT a safe use of the square knot because it can slip and become untied when a load is placed on it, especially if it capsizes. For this purpose, a better choice might be the double fisherman's knot or sheet bend which are both described later in this book.

Pros: This knot is extremely simple to tie and untie.
Cons: As previously mentioned, this is a knot that can become untied when a load is placed on the working ends of the rope, which can result in serious injury and/or death when used in certain circumstances. When this knot isn't under tension, it can sometimes shake loose and become untied.

How to tie it:
1. While holding an end of rope in each hand, cross the working end of the rope in your right hand over the working end of the rope in your left hand, making an "x." This is illustrated in figure 18a. The working end of

the rope from your right hand is now on the left side and the working end of the rope from your left hand is on the right side.

Figure 18a.

2. Wrap the working end of the rope from your right hand behind and under the working end of the rope from your left hand as illustrated in figure 18b.

Figure 18b.

3. Continue wrapping this working end until it lies over the working end of the rope from your left hand. This is illustrated in figure 18c.

Figure 18c.

4. Next, take the working end that is on the left side and cross it over the working end of the rope on the right side, making another "x" as illustrated in figure 18d.

5. Wrap the working end of the rope from your left hand behind and under the working end of the rope from your right hand.

Figure 18d.

6. Continue wrapping this working end until it lies over the working end of the rope from your right hand as illustrated in figure 18e.

Figure 18e.

7. You'll now have a working end and a standing part in each hand. Pull them away from each other to make the

Figure 18f.

knot tight and you have completed a square knot. The completed knot is illustrated in figure 18f.

Note: An easy way to remember how to tie this knot is by reciting a simple mnemonic phrase which goes, "Right over left, left over right, then pull the knot tidy and tight."

It's worth pointing out that if you tie this knot incorrectly, you'll end up with what is known as a "granny knot." Even with the limitations of the square knot, it's still better than a granny knot. It's quite easy to tell if you tied a granny or a square knot. You do this by looking at each side of the knot. If you tied the square knot correctly, the left side should have a working end and the standing part under a bight. The right side should have a working end and the standing part over a bight. Figure 19 shows what the knot will look like if you tied it incorrectly and actually tied a granny knot.

Figure 19.

Possible Uses:

1. If you are treating a wound and you're in need of a knot to secure a bandage to a limb such as an arm or leg, a square knot may be a good choice.

2. While collecting branches and twigs for a fire, this knot can be used to bind the bundle together for carrying it back to your camp.

3. When in need of a makeshift belt, a length of rope can be tied around your waist using a square knot to help keep your pants up. This could be especially useful if you find yourself in a prolonged survival situation where you end up losing weight and have a difficult time keeping your pants from falling down.

Bowline

This is a go-to knot for many preppers. When people need to tie a loop in the end of a rope or they need to secure a rope around something, a bowline is often used.

Pros: This knot is easy to tie and untie, plus it's fairly secure. When there is a load on the line, a bowline has a tendency to tighten down upon itself, making the knot even tighter. Another benefit of a bowline is that the loop won't constrict around the item it is tied around when tension is applied to the standing part of the rope.

Cons: A negative characteristic of this particular knot is that if the rope isn't under tension, the knot can sometimes be shaken loose. One of the pros of this knot can also be a con. When there is tension on the rope, it can be difficult, if not impossible, to tie or untie this knot.

How to tie it:

1. Form an overhand loop in the standing part as illustrated in figure 20a.

Figure 20a.

2. Pass the working end up through the loop as illustrated in figure 20b.

Figure 20b.

3. Wrap the working end behind the standing part as illustrated in figure 20c.

Figure 20c.

4. Thread the working end back down through the over-hand loop you tied in step 1 as illustrated in figure 20d.

Figure 20d.

5. Dress the knot and pull it tight to complete the bowline. Figure 20e shows what this knot should look like but note

Figure 20e.

that for illustration purposes, it hasn't been tightened in the photo.

Note: Many people remind themselves about how to tie this knot by reciting the simple mnemonic phrase, "The rabbit pops out of its hole, runs behind and around the tree, and scurries back into its hole." The rabbit popping out of its hole would be step 2, running behind and around the tree would be step 3, and scurrying back into its hole would be step 4.

Possible Uses:

1. There are almost too many uses for a bowline to mention. As noted in the description about this particular knot, it is often used when a loop is needed that won't constrict and get tight around the item it is tied to. If you've ever tried to tie a loop in the end of a rope only to have it constrict around the item it's tied to, or if your knot becomes untied when you pull on the standing end, you may want to consider using a bowline.

2. This knot can be used for tying a loop in the end of a rope that will be used to secure a tent guy line.

3. If you have the need to tie a raft or canoe to a tree while floating on a river, you can use the bowline to securely tether your boat.

One-Handed Bowline

There is a variation of the bowline known as the "one-handed bowline." This is very handy if you ever need to quickly tie a bowline around your waist.

It's very simple to tie but quite difficult to describe with words and pictures. To help you understand the steps, the rabbit mnemonic phrase that is often used to remember how to tie a bowline will be used in the following instructions. Keep in mind as you're viewing the photographs that the rope is wrapped around my body and I'm tying the knot with my right hand only.

How to tie it:

1. Take hold of the working end and pass it around your waist so the standing part is on the left side of your body and the working end is on the right side of your body. This is illustrated in figure 21a.

Figure 21a.

2. Make sure your right hand is holding the working end, leaving approximately seven or eight inches of rope between the end and the position where you are holding the rope.

3. With the working end in your right hand, cross it over the standing part that is on the left side of your body. This is illustrated in figure 21b.

Figure 21b.

4. Bend your right wrist and with a twisting motion, go over the standing part and towards your belly button. This is illustrated in figure 21c.

Figure 21c.

5. Hook the standing part with your thumb as illustrated in figure 21d.

Figure 21d.

6. Continue using a twisting motion with your right hand and you'll end up with an overhand loop around your hand and the working end on the right hand side of the standing part as illustrated in figure 21e. This loop is like the one you created in step 1 of tying a standard bowline except your hand and the working end will be inside the loop. You might think of this step as the "rabbit popping out of its hole."

Figure 21e.

7. Now the rabbit needs to go "behind and around the tree." With your index finger, pass the working end behind the standing part to the left as illustrated in figure 21f.

Figure 21f.

8. Use your thumb to hook the working end to bring it "around the tree." This is illustrated in figure 21g.

Figure 21g.

9. Now that the rabbit has made it around the tree, grab the working end and pull it through the loop. With this step, you've essentially made the rabbit "scurry back into its hole." Figure 21h shows what the knot should look like after you've pulled the working end through the hole.

Figure 21h.

10. Pull the knot tight and you've completed the one-handed bowline. You can see how the finished bowline will
be around your waist illustrated in figure 21i.

Figure 21i.

Possible Uses:

1. Imagine you are taking a canoe on a river and it capsizes.
Suddenly you find yourself being swept down the river
when someone on the bank sees you and throws you a
rope. Even if the current isn't swift, it may be quite difficult to hold on to the end of a rope, especially when it's
wet. If you know how to tie the one-handed bowline,

you may be able to quickly tie it around your waist so rescuers can pull you to shore.

2. Imagine another scenario where you happen to be hiking on steep ground and you suddenly slip and find yourself precariously perched on a rock ledge. Maybe you're holding onto a rock or a tree with one hand to keep from falling when someone throws you a rope that doesn't already have a bowline tied in it. If you know how to tie the one-handed version, you may be able to secure the rope around your waist so the people who threw the rope can pull you up.

Note: One thing that can't be overstated regarding this knot is to *practice, practice, practice!* You should practice this one so much that it becomes as easy as tying your shoelaces. In an emergency, you're going to have to rely on your muscle memory and instincts to tie this knot. Otherwise, fear will likely prevent you from remembering the steps described in this book. So, in case you didn't get the point, practice tying this knot hundreds of times and then practice tying it some more. *Someday, it could save your life!*

Double Fisherman's Knot

There will undoubtedly be times when you'll need to take two lengths of rope and tie them together to make one longer rope. The double fisherman's knot, which is sometimes referred to as the "grapevine knot," is often used for this purpose. It's an interesting knot because it's actually two knots that, when a load is applied to the rope, lock onto each other. One way to think about it is that you are tying two stopper knots that work in unison to prevent the other from sliding through it. Ironically enough, this knot isn't actually often used by fishermen.

Pros: Due to the nature of the way this knot is tied, it is often the knot of choice for tying two lengths of rope together. Many believe that this is a more secure knot for this purpose than some of the other knots commonly used to join multiple lengths of rope.

Cons: After a heavy load has been placed on a rope that has a double fisherman's knot tied in it, the knot can be extremely difficult to untie. This one can also be a little tricky to tie so it's critical for you to pay very close attention to make sure the rope is lying neat and tidy while you dress the knot and before you tighten it.

How to tie it:

1. Lay the working ends of each rope parallel to each other with the ends overlapping by a few inches as illustrated in figure 22a. The diameter of your rope will determine how much this overlap needs to be. As you practice tying the double fisherman's knot, you'll develop a feel for how

long the overlapping sections should be. You'll need less of an overlap when using thin rope like paracord but more when using thick rope.

Figure 22a.

2. Cross the working end on the right side over the standing part and wrap it behind and around to the top as illustrated in figure 22b. You'll see that you've created a wrap around the standing part and the place where the wrap is now lying looks like the letter "x."

Figure 22b.

3. Make another wrap, keeping this one on the left side of the "x" you just formed. This is illustrated in figure 22c.

Figure 22c.

4. Thread the working end through both wraps as illustrated in figure 22d. You'll actually be threading it under the "x" towards the right.

Figure 22d.

5. Dress this knot and pull it tight. At this point you have completed the first half of this knot.

6. Now it's time to repeat the process on the other length of rope. Cross the working end that is on the left over the standing part. Make a wrap around this standing part by passing the working end behind this standing part. At the completion of this step, the working end will be facing downwards. This is illustrated in figure 22e. You'll see that you've created a wrap around the standing part.and the place where the wrap is now lying looks like the letter "x."

Figure 22e.

7. Make another wrap, keeping this one on the right side of the "x" you just formed as illustrated in figure 22f.

Figure 22f.

8. Thread the working end through both wraps. You'll actually be threading it under the "x" towards the left.

9. Dress this knot and pull it tight as illustrated in figure 22g. You have now completed the second half of this knot.

Figure 22g.

10. While this might sound a little confusing, you've now actually tied two double fisherman's knots, one on each of the standing parts.

11. To complete the double fisherman's knot, simply pull on each standing part and the fisherman's knots will slide together. The finished knot will look like the one in figure 22h.

Figure 22h.

Note: If you've tied this knot correctly it will appear very neat and tidy. You'll have two knots next to each other that each look like an "x" when viewing it from one side. If you flip it over, the two knots will look like four diagonal parallel lines. The working ends should be on opposite diagonals of the knot as well. If they are both on the same side, you've made a mistake and need to start over.

Variation: Some people make an extra wrap before threading the working end under the "x." in each fisherman's knot. This will result in a knot commonly referred to as the "triple fisherman's knot."

Possible Uses:

1. Tying two or more lengths of rope together to make one longer length of rope. This may come in really handy if you ever have to scavenge for cordage.

2. Anytime you want to tie both ends of a rope together to form a loop, you can use a double fisherman's knot.

Sheet Bend

Many people use this knot when they have two ropes of different diameters that they need to join together. Joining two ropes of varying diameters is this knot's claim to fame but you can also use it to connect ropes of the same diameter. By the way, it's also known as the "weaver's knot" in some circles.

Pros: Tying a knot using differing diameters of rope can sometimes make the knot unstable and prone to slipping, but this knot is specifically designed for this purpose.

Cons: It may have a tendency to work its way loose if tension isn't kept on the two ropes.

How to tie it:

1. Make a bight with the working end of the thicker diameter rope and hold it in your left hand as illustrated in figure 23a.

Figure 23a.

2. Keep the "u" in the bight facing towards the right and the working end at the top of the bight.

3. Holding the thinner rope in your right hand, thread it up from the bottom of the "u" in the bight as illustrated in figure 23b.

Figure 23b.

4. Pass the working end of the thinner rope behind and around the bight. It's important to start this wrap towards the top of the knot, or in other words, towards the direction the working end of the bight is facing. This is illustrated in figure 23c.

Figure 23c.

5. Thread the working end of the thinner rope under itself as illustrated in figure 23d.

Figure 23d.

6. Dress and tighten the knot to complete the sheet bend. The finished knot should look like the one shown in figure 23e.

Figure 23e.

Note: If you don't follow these steps correctly, you'll end up with the working end of both ropes on the opposite sides of the knot. This will result in an incorrectly tied sheet bend which is more likely to slip than one that is tied correctly. When properly tied, the working ends will both be oriented towards the top of the knot.

Possible Uses:

If the rope you need to use isn't long enough, you can use this knot to fasten two or more lengths of rope together. This is especially handy if you ever have to resort to scavenging for rope and you don't have the luxury of each piece of rope being the same type and diameter.

Double Sheet Bend

A slight modification to the sheet bend will result in a "double sheet bend" which is supposed to be more secure.

How to tie it:

1. Make a bight with the working end of the thicker diameter rope and hold it in your left hand as illustrated in figure 23a.

2. Keep the "u" in the bight facing towards the right and the working end at the top of the bight.

3. Holding the thinner rope in your right hand, thread it up from the bottom of the "u" in the bight as illustrated in figure 23b.

4. Pass the working end of the thinner rope behind and around the bight. It's important to start this wrap towards the top of the knot, or in other words, towards the direction the working end of the bight is facing. This is illustrated in figure 23c.

5. Thread the working end of the thinner rope under itself as illustrated in figure 23d.

6. Repeat steps 4 and 5 to make a second wrap.

7. Dress and tighten the knot to complete the double sheet bend. The finished knot should look like the one illustrated in figure 24.

Figure 24.

Possible Uses:

You can use this knot in the same manner in which you use a sheet bend but in situations where you want a knot that is a bit more secure.

Prusik Knot

This knot, which is also sometimes referred to as the "prusik hitch," is very handy when you have a length of rope and you would like to attach something to the standing part of the rope. In order for this knot to function properly, it should be tied with thinner rope than the main rope it is attached to.

Pros: One can easily attach a prusik knot to a rope that is already under tension. It is useful because when a load or tension is applied to it, friction helps prevent it from sliding on the main rope. When the tension is removed, the prusik knot can easily be slid to another position along the rope.

Cons: This is another knot where one of the positive characteristics can also be a negative one. This is because the knot can be unintentionally moved from the position that it was originally tied onto the main line if tension isn't kept applied to the knot. This knot may also be prone to slipping if the rope you are using happens to be wet or icy since there won't likely be enough friction to hold the knot in place.

Again, remembering that this knot relies on the friction between the two knots to hold it in place, it can be more or less effective depending upon the type of rope used.

How to tie it:

1. Decide how large you would like the loop to be. This is determined by the number of times you would like to wrap the loop around the main rope. More wraps will of course require a larger loop. This will make more sense as you continue reading about how this knot is used.

2. Cut a length of rope several inches longer than you want the overall diameter of the loop to be.

3. Tie the ends together with a double fisherman's knot. You'll now have a loop like the one illustrated in figure 25a.

Figure 25a.

4. Lay the loop behind the main rope as illustrated in figure 25b.

Figure 25b.

5. Pass the end with the fisherman's knot in the loop over and around the thicker rope. The double fisherman's knot should actually pass through the loop so that your loop of rope is now wrapped completely around the thicker rope. This is illustrated in figure 25c.

Figure 25c.

6. Thread this end through the loop at least three times. Pay close attention as you make each wrap so the coils in the wraps don't cross over each other.

7. You will have now created at least three wraps around the thicker main rope. Take a minute and dress the knot to double-check that all of these wraps are lying neatly and not crossing over each other. Figure 25d shows three wraps of the loop around the main line and they are all neatly dressed.

8. Apply tension to the end of the rope with the fisherman's knot in it to take the slack out of the knot. You have now completed the prusik knot. Note that you'll have to manipulate the wraps with your fingers somewhat to get them to snug up tightly around the main line. Figure 25e shows what the completed prusik knot should look like on the main line.

Figure 25d.

If you have tied it correctly, and you are using rope with enough friction, you shouldn't be able to move the position of the prusik knot along the standing part of the thicker rope when tension is applied to

Figure 25e.

the loop laterally. The beautiful thing about this knot is that if you simply grab the entire knot at the position in which it is attached to the thicker rope when the loop doesn't have tension applied to it, you can easily slide it to reposition it. As soon as tension is applied to the loop, the prusik knot should once again hold tight to the thicker rope and maintain its position.

Possible Uses:

1. This knot is sometimes used in mountaineering. If you choose to use this knot for mountaineering purposes, be sure to get training on how to properly do so from a qualified instructor.

2. If you have horses or mules, you can secure them to a high-line rope with a prusik knot. Simply attach a tight ridgeline between two trees, then attach prusik knots at various intervals along the highline. The nature of this knot makes it easy to reposition it on the highline to evenly space each animal out. When you have the prusik knot where you want it, tie their lead rope to the loop in the prusik. If they try to pull towards either end of the highline, the friction produced by this knot is supposed to prevent it from sliding along the rope and it should keep them in position.

3. If you have to make a shelter with a tarp draped over a rope ridgeline, you can position a prusik knot on each end of the ridgeline to keep the tarp stretched tight.

4. The prusik is a handy knot designed so that it shouldn't slip along the main thicker rope it is tied to but unlike some knots, it only functions properly when tension is maintained on the loop. Always keep this in mind when using this knot.

Warning: It's very important to properly train horses or mules to stand calmly when they are tied to a highline. Working with large animals can be extremely dangerous so this isn't something you should do unless both you and your animals have been properly trained to use a highline. Even then, there is risk and danger associated with this activity.

Two Half Hitch

Many people call this knot a "double half hitch" simply because it's tied, like the name implies, by tying two half hitches. As described earlier in this book, a half hitch is simply an overhand knot that is tied around something. It is a binding knot used for the purpose of attaching cordage to an object such as a tree. One half hitch by itself under tension isn't nearly as secure as when you tie a two half hitch knot. This knot is also often used as a way of finishing or locking down more complex knots.

Pros: This very basic binding knot has a tendency to constrict around the object it is tied to when tension is applied to the standing part. The fact that this knot will usually constrict around the object it is tied to makes it a good choice for applications when you don't want the knot to move from the original position in which it was tied. This is, of course, only if there is adequate friction between the rope and the object the knot is tied around.

Cons: Ironically, the fact that this knot does constrict around the object it is tied to can sometimes actually be a disadvantage. It's important to remember that this knot can slide on the standing part, and for it to function properly it should be slid all the way towards the object that it's tied to. If you don't want the loop that this knot creates to constrict around an object, consider using a knot such as the bowline or even the figure 8 follow-through knot.

How to tie it:

1. With the working end in your hand, pass it around an object such as a tree or pole thereby forming a single turn as illustrated in figure 26a.

Figure 26a.

2. Next pass the working end in front of the standing part as illustrated in figure 26b.

3. Thread the working end through the loop you created and pull the first half hitch tight as illustrated in figure 26c. Note that this is simply an overhand knot that is tied around something.

4. Pass the working end around the standing part again, but this time the wrap should be on the outside of the loop. This is illustrated in figure 26d.

5. Threading the working end through the second loop you just created forms the second half hitch.

Figure 26b.

Figure 26c.

6. Dress the knot before pulling both half hitches tight and you have completed the two half hitch. The finished knot should look like the one that you see in figure 26e.

Figure 26d.

Possible Uses:

1. If you're hanging a hammock between two trees and you want to attach the ends of the ropes to the trees, the two half hitch knot may be a good choice. Because this knot can constrict around the tree, friction will be produced between the rope and the tree bark which may help to prevent the hitch from sliding down the tree while you are lying in the hammock.

Figure 26e.

2. If you are constructing a simple shelter made with a tarp, this knot can be used to attach an end of the rope to a grommet in the tarp.

3. This knot can also be used to attach the guylines on a tent to a rainfly.

Two Half Hitch with a Bight

A handy variation of the two half hitch just described is the two half hitch with a bight. Read on to discover what makes this one special. Keep in mind that due to the nature in which this knot is tied, it shouldn't be used in critical applications. However, if you just need a knot that's quick and easy to both tie and untie, it might be a good choice.

Pros: This knot is similar to the two half hitch described above but it's much quicker and easier to untie.
Cons: The fact that this knot is quicker and easier to untie presents the possibility that it could become untied when you don't intend it to. With this in mind, remember that this variation isn't as secure.

How to tie it:

1. With the working end in your hand, pass it around an object such as a tree or pole thereby forming a single turn as illustrated in figure 26a.

2. Next, pass the working end in front of the standing part as illustrated in figure 26b.

3. Thread the working end through the loop you created and pull the first half hitch tight as illustrated in figure 26c. Note that this is simply an overhand knot that is tied around something.

4. Form a bight with the remaining section of your working end. This is the step that makes this knot easier to untie. Pass the bight around the standing part, but this time the wrap should be on the outside of the loop. This is illustrated in figure 27a.

Figure 27a.

5. Threading the bight through the second loop you just created forms the second half hitch.

6. Dress the knot before pulling both half hitches

Figure 27b.

tight and you have completed the round turn and two half hitch with a bight knot. The finished knot should look like the one you see in figure 27b.

Possible Uses:
You can use this knot for similar applications in which the two half hitch is used. However, this variation can be quite useful when it comes to untying the knot. All you have to do is grab hold of the working end and pull on it. This will pull the bight through the second half hitch and untie it. Doing this will make it possible to untie the entire knot much more quickly.

Round Turn and Two Half Hitch Knot
This might be considered a variation of the two half hitch knot but its added usefulness warrants its own section in this book.

Pros: There is more friction applied to the tree or any other anchor point you might choose to tie this knot to. This should help reduce slipping and spread the weight of the load on the rope over two turns instead of just one. This may make the knot stronger and less likely to break.
Cons: It takes slightly longer to tie and untie this variation but the added strength of the knot probably makes up for the added time.

How to tie it:

1. Instead of doing a single turn around a stationary object as described in step one of the instructions for tying the two half hitch, you pass the rope around the object again forming a complete round turn as illustrated in figure 28a.

2. Next, pass the working end in front of the standing part as illustrated in figure 28b.

Figure 28a.

Figure 28b.

3. Thread the working end through the loop you created and pull the first half hitch tight as illustrated in figure 28c.

4. Pass the working end around the standing part again, but this time the wrap should be on the outside of the loop. This is illustrated in figure 28d.

5. Threading the working end through the second loop you just created forms the second half hitch.

Figure 28c.

6. Dress the knot before pulling both half hitches tight and you have completed the two half hitch. The finished knot should look like the one you see in figure 28e.

Possible Uses:

1. This knot is useful anytime you want to secure a rope to a stationary object. Many of the same situations where you

Figure 28d.

might use the two half hitch apply to this knot, but it also has the added benefit of having more surface area of the round turn to create more friction, which may result in an overall stronger knot.

Figure 28e.

2. Tying your boat to a cleat on a dock may be a good use for this knot.

Midshipman's Hitch

This is a useful knot for occasions when you have a length of rope securing something to an anchor point and you may need to adjust the tension on the rope. Once tied, you can easily slide this knot along the main rope to increase or decrease tension. When a load is applied to the standing part, the knot is designed to stay in position without slipping due to friction created between the knot and the rope.

It's worth pointing out that there is a variant of this knot commonly known as a "tautline hitch." The two knots are similar and have the same use but some consider the midshipman's hitch to be more secure.

Regardless of which variation you choose to use, neither of them are a good choice for applications when you need to put a considerable amount of tension on the line. For this application, you might want to use the trucker's hitch which is described later in this book. However, if you just want a knot you can use to quickly add or remove tension from a rope on something like a tent guyline, the midshipman's hitch might be a good choice.

Pros: It's easy to make quick adjustments to guylines that have a midshipman's hitch tied in them. Unlike the bowline, this knot can actually be tied when there is already a load on the standing part of the rope.

Cons: This knot relies on friction to keep it from sliding on the standing part of the rope. If a midshipman's hitch is tied on rope that is slippery in nature, it will most likely not hold its position on the main standing part of the rope due to the lack of friction.

Figure 29a.

How to tie it:

1. Make a turn with the working end around your desired anchor point as illustrated in figure 29a.

2. Cross the working end over the standing part as illustrated in figure 29b.

Figure 29b.

3. Wrap the working end under and around the standing part, making sure your wrap is on the inside of the loop. This is illustrated in figure 29c.

4. Continue to wrap the working end around the first turn making sure to cross over the first turn,

Figure 29c.

keeping this second turn in the part of the loop closest to you as illustrated in figure 29d. This second turn forms an "x" over the first turn that creates additional friction, thereby making it a more secure knot than the tautline hitch.

5. Apply tension to the working end to prevent the knot from slipping while you complete the midshipman's hitch.

Figure 29d.

6. Continue wrapping with the working end but this time on the outside of the loop. Pass the working end behind the standing part as illustrated in figure 29e.

7. Thread the working end through the hole in this wrap. What you're actually doing in this step is tying a

Figure 29e.

half hitch on the outside of the loop around the standing part. Figure 29f shows this step before the half hitch is tightened.

8. Dress the knot, pull it tight, and you have completed a midshipman's hitch. Note that in order for this knot to function properly, you must get it tight before you apply a load to it. The finished knot should look like the one that you see in figure 29g.

Figure 29f.

How to adjust it:

Simply grab the knot in your hand and slide it either up the standing part to make the loop bigger (creating more tension

Figure 29g.

on the line) or down the standing part to make it smaller (reducing the tension on the line). You should understand that if there is too much tension on the sanding part of the rope, it could be quite difficult, or even impossible, to slide the knot up the rope towards the working end. On the other hand, regardless of how much tension is on the standing part, it's usually fairly easy to slide the knot towards the anchor point if you want to reduce the tension on the line.

Possible Uses:

1. This knot is a great choice for attaching guylines to tent stakes because after the knot is tied, you can easily slide it up the standing part to apply tension to the guyline. When you want to take your tent down, simply slide the knot towards the anchor point to release the tension on the guyline.

2. You can also use this knot to secure one end of a rope to a tree when putting up a ridgeline for a tarp shelter. After you tie one end of your rope to a tree, simply tie a midshipman's hitch to a tree at the other end of your ridgeline. Then, while holding onto the standing part of the rope, slide the knot towards the other tree. Using this method, you will be able to make your ridgeline tight, which will help prevent your tarp shelter from sagging.

3. You can use this same technique to create a makeshift clothesline.

Trucker's Hitch

This is a knot virtually everyone can use. It has many practical applications in survival situations but also in day to day living. If you ever need to secure a load to something like a trailer or even to the roof rack of your car, you might want to consider tying a trucker's hitch.

For those of you who don't already know about this knot, you've probably experienced how difficult it can be to securely tie something to the roof rack on your car or to a trailer. Most people will pull and pull to get the rope tight, but when they tie a knot they lose the tension and the load is no longer tightly secured.

A trucker's hitch is designed to make use of mechanical advantage similar to the way a pulley or block and tackle work to apply tension to the rope that is securing the load. Due to the way it is tied, the tension on the rope isn't lost when the knot is tied. It performs similarly to ratchet straps, but instead of using a mechanical device to tighten nylon webbing, you are using rope and a really useful knot.

Pros: If tied properly, this knot isn't likely to slip and should therefore maintain tension on the object(s) it is securing. Also, because of the fact that there is the benefit of mechanical advantage when tying this knot, it's possible to get the rope you are using to secure an object tighter than if you were just pulling on the rope and tying it off with a couple of half hitches.

Cons: There are a couple of variations of this knot. One makes use of a loop that is designed to be easy to untie. The other utilizes a "fixed loop" which some people believe makes the knot more secure. While it may be more secure, it's also more difficult to untie the loop after a load has been applied to it. Additionally, if you use the same rope many times to secure objects, the friction the loop is subjected to could cause a weak spot to develop in your rope. Eventually, the rope could break at this weak spot. For this reason, you will be instructed how to tie a trucker's hitch using the "slip loop" method.

How to tie it:

While not actually part of the trucker's hitch, you will need to have the standing end of your rope tied to a stationary anchor point using a knot like a bowline or two half hitch before you tie this knot. One possible example of an anchor point might be the roof rack on your car.

1. Make an overhand loop somewhere along the standing part of your rope as illustrated in figure 30a. After you learn to tie a trucker's hitch, you'll develop a pretty good

idea of where this loop should be positioned and why it's important to choose the location for this loop carefully.

Figure 30a.

2. Make a bight with the length of rope that is towards the working end as illustrated in figure 30b.

Figure 30b.

3. Thread the bight into the overhand loop from the under-side as illustrated in figure 30c.

Figure 30c.

4. Keeping a firm grasp on "u" in the bight, pull on both the working end and standing part. This will create a "slip

Figure 30d.

loop" in your rope that can easily be untied when you want to use the rope for something else in the future. Essentially, this is just an overhand knot with a bight in it. Figure 30d illustrates this step.

5. Now take the working end and make a single turn around a stationary object to act as an opposing anchor point to the one the standing end is tied to.

6. Pass the working end through the loop you created in step 4.

7. Pull the working end towards the anchor point you wrapped the rope around in step 5 as illustrated in figure 30e. The wrap around the anchor point from step 5 and threading the working end through the loop in this step is similar to a block and tackle. This is what provides

Figure 30e.

the mechanical advantage that makes it possible to apply tension to secure a load to something.

8. Pull on the working end until you are satisfied with the amount of tension on the rope.

9. When you feel like you have enough tension on the rope, use your thumb and index finger to pinch the rope at the point where the working end crosses over the loop. This will keep the hitch from slipping and you from losing tension on the rope while you finish tying the knot.

10. To lock this hitch down, simply tie a two half hitch knot around both lengths of rope that are secured to your opposing anchor point described in step 5. This step is illustrated in figure 30f.

Figure 30f.

11. Dress the half hitches, tighten them, and you have completed the trucker's hitch.

One thing to remember is that you will need to carefully consider where you tie the slip loop in your rope as described in step 4. If you tie it too close to the anchor point described in step 5, you won't have enough room to pull the hitch tight and, consequently, you won't be able to apply tension to the object you are trying to secure. On the other hand, if you tie it too far away from the opposing anchor point, you might not have enough rope to pass the working end around the anchor, through the slip loop, and still complete the two half hitch to lock the knot down tight.

Possible Uses:

1. We discussed using a midshipman's hitch to set up a ridgeline earlier, but a trucker's hitch might be an even better choice for this application. You'll be able to get your ridgeline considerably tighter with the mechanical advantage a trucker's hitch provides.

2. We also discussed setting up a highline and prusik knots to tie horses or mules to at a campsite. The trucker's hitch might also be good for this.

3. If you are attaching something like a canoe to the roof rack of your car or truck, this knot might be a good option.

4. It can also be used to secure a load to a trailer or the bed of your pickup truck.

Clove Hitch

A clove hitch is a simple, but handy knot that is often used to attach a rope to an object in *non-critical applications*. This knot relies on the friction of the wraps to hold it in place. Great care and consideration was taken in regards to whether this hitch should be included in this book. Ultimately, it was included because, even with its limitations, it does have some practical applications.

Pros: It is very quick and easy to tie and untie.
Cons: Due to its simplicity, this knot can often be prone to slipping and/or capsizing. It has several useful purposes but *it shouldn't be trusted as the single knot in critical applications*. Additionally, if you tie a clove hitch on something and tension isn't maintained in the correct direction, the wraps in this knot can capsize and the knot can become untied.

It's important to understand that a clove hitch is a directional knot. When tying it, you'll be wrapping the rope around an object in a particular direction. The friction that holds the knot together will only be maintained if tension is pulled in the correct direction. If you apply tension in the wrong direction, the knot will capsize and become untied.

You can easily test this for yourself by tying a clove hitch and then pulling on the standing part of the rope in the correct direction. If the hitch was tied correctly and there is enough friction between the rope and the object you secured it to, it should hold fast. Now, if you pull on the standing part in the opposite direction, you'll see this hitch quickly capsize and become untied.

How to tie it:

1. Wrap the working end of your rope around a stationary object, such as a post or tree, completing a single turn as illustrated in figure 31a.

Figure 31a.

2. Continue wrapping, and with this second turn you should cross over the first turn as illustrated in figure 31b. Crossing over this first turn will create an "x" where the ropes cross.

3. Thread the working end under the second wrap as illustrated in figure 31c.

Figure 31b.

Figure 31c.

4. Dress the knot and pull the working end and standing part in opposite directions to complete the clove hitch. The finished knot should look like the one you see in figure 31d.

Figure 31d.

Variation: Adding either an overhand knot or a figure 8 knot as a stopper to the working end of the clove hitch as illustrated in figure 9 may sometimes help to prevent slipping. However, even with the addition of a stopper knot, the clove hitch should still be used with great caution.

Possible Uses:

1. In non-critical applications, the clove hitch can be used to fasten one end of a length of cordage to a stationary object. Objects such as tree branches that have enough bark to aid in creating friction are usually best suited for this knot.

2. If you're making a shelter using scavenged tree limbs, a clove hitch can be a useful knot to start and end any lashings you might use to bind the branches to each other.

Constrictor Knot

By making a very slight modification to the way you tie a clove hitch, you'll end up with a constrictor knot. Many people, including the author, prefer this to the clove hitch. As a matter of fact, this is one of the author's favorite knots!

Pros: Much like the clove hitch, this is a quick and easy knot to tie. The advantage is that it gets tighter as you apply more tension and it's less prone to slipping and collapsing.

Cons: One of the negative characteristics of this particular knot is that it can be quite difficult to untie after it has really been cinched down tight. This seems to be especially true with smaller diameter cordage.

How to tie it:

1. Wrap the working end of your rope around a stationary object such as a post or tree, completing a single turn as illustrated in figure 31a.

2. Continue wrapping, but with this second turn you should cross over the first turn as illustrated in figure 31b. Crossing over this first turn will create an "x" where the ropes cross.

3. Pass the working end over the standing part and thread it under the "x" as illustrated in figure 32a. The fact that the working end passes over the standing part and then under the "x" is what makes this knot different than the clove hitch. If you didn't pass it over the standing part before threading it under the "x," you would end up with a less secure clove hitch.

Figure 32a.

4. Dress the knot and pull the working end and standing part in the opposite directions to complete the constrictor hitch. The finished knot should

Figure 32b.

look like the one you see in figure 32b. Note the subtle, but important, difference between figure 31d and 32b.

Alternate method of tying:

There is another way of tying this knot that is very handy if you want it to be in the middle of a length of rope instead of at the working end.

1. Lay your rope down so that it forms an "s" shape as illustrated in figure 33a. Essentially, you have two bights with the "u" shape of the bights pointing in opposite directions.

Figure 33a.

2. Grasp the "u" in the bights and rotate them in a counterclockwise direction so that your rope looks like the number 8. This step is illustrated in figure 33b.

3. With one hand, pinch the center of the "8" and hold it.

4. With your other hand, fold the two loops downward until they touch as illustrated in figure 33c.

Figure 33b.

5. Now you have a constrictor knot that hasn't been tied around anything or tightened down yet.

6. Place the two loops of the knot around the object you want to

Figure 33c.

bind and pull on both ends of the rope. An example of using the constrictor knot to bind a coiled hank of rope is illustrated in figure 33d. Note that unlike the knot in figure 32d that is tied with the working end of the rope, this constrictor knot is tied in the middle of the standing part of the rope.

Figure 33d.

Possible Uses:

1. The author and her family tie this knot all the time using string as a replacement for commonly used plastic cable ties.

2. If you have items like sticks that you have collected for firewood, a constrictor knot can be used to keep them bundled tightly together.

3. When you need to secure something to the frame of a backpack, this knot may come in very handy.

4. Like the square knot, the constrictor knot can be used to secure a bandage or a splint to an injured limb. Just use caution to make sure you don't apply too much tension when tightening the knot or you might restrict the blood circulation, which could result in permanent damage and possibly even the need to have the limb amputated. If you choose to use this knot to apply a bandage or splint to someone, be sure to monitor the person frequently to ensure the knot isn't so tight that it is restricting blood circulation. If you discover that it is, you should probably loosen the knot to prevent any medical complications.

5. This knot is great for keeping a coiled up rope or an extension cord tightly bound so that it isn't a tangled mess when you need to use it.

Poacher's Knot

If you find yourself in a survival situation where you have to resort to trying to trap some small animals to put food on the table, you'll be glad you know how to tie this knot. It creates a noose you might be able to use to snare some game with. This knot is also sometimes referred to as the "poacher's snare" or "strangle snare."

Pros: This knot is easy to tie and when the loop this knot creates is pulled on, it locks down tight. This means if you trap an animal with it, the harder they pull, the tighter it gets.

Cons: The knot is designed to easily tighten but once tightened, you may have to cut the cordage because it can be quite difficult to loosen the noose.

How to tie it:

1. Pass the working end over the standing part to create a loop as illustrated in figure 34a.

Figure 34a.

2. Pinch the section where the working end crosses over the standing part with your thumb and index finger.

3. Make a wrap with the working end around the loop as illustrated in figure 34b. Note that the spot where the working end crosses over itself in this step creates an "x".

Figure 34b.

4. Make another partial wrap with the working end around the loop as illustrated in figure 34c. Keep this wrap towards the loop and not the standing end. In this step, you don't need to make a complete wrap, just pass the working end behind the standing part as figure 34c illustrates.

Figure 34c.

5. Stop pinching the rope and thread the working end through both wraps as illustrated in figure 34d. You'll actually be threading the working end under the "x" that you created in step 3.

Figure 34d.

6. Gently pull on the working end, making sure that you don't tighten the knot all the way, and you have completed the poacher's knot. You have effectively tied a special type of slip knot. The knot should easily slide on the standing part at this point if you've tied it correctly. If it doesn't, you tightened it too tightly. The finished knot should look like the one that you see in figure 34e.

Possible Uses:

1. As previously mentioned, this knot can be used to set snares to catch small game. If you choose to use it for this purpose, it's critical that you don't overly tighten the knot in step 6. By leaving the knot that is tied around the standing part loose, it will be able to quickly and smoothly slide along the standing part so that it easily constricts around the animal that runs through your snare. When the animal feels this noose tighten, it will struggle in an attempt to free itself and the knot will tighten, making it difficult, if not impossible, for the animal to escape.

2. It can also be used as a binding knot if you alter step 6 and actually tighten the knot around the standing part. One possible use might be to tie a poacher's knot in two lengths of paracord. Then, after you roll up your sleeping bag or pad, you can place the loop of each rope around your bedding. When you pull on the standing end, the knot will constrict and hold tight, thereby keeping your bedding neatly rolled up. When you need to unroll it, simply pinch the knot and give it a good pull to slide it up the standing part, which will loosen the noose you used to bind your bedroll.

Note: If you choose to use this knot for snaring animals, make sure to follow all applicable laws pertaining to trapping in your area. Also, please be a responsible trapper and check on your traps frequently so that you can humanely dispatch any animal that may become entangled in your snare. In a life or death survival situation, it may be necessary to trap animals to feed your family and stay alive but the utmost care should be taken to do all you can to ensure that no animals suffer.

Bonus Section: Fishing Knots

The next portion of this book will provide instructions for tying some commonly used fishing knots. Many preppers plan to incorporate fishing to provide a potential source of food while trying to survive the aftermath of a major catastrophe. If you're one of them, learning to tie these popular fishing knots will be well worth your time and effort.

It's worth pointing out that even if you've done quite well while learning how to tie the knots discussed so far, you may struggle a bit with the knots in this section. For the purpose of making the individual steps easier to illustrate in the photographs, fishing line isn't used. Instead, paracord is used for demonstration purposes only. It's okay if you want to practice these knots using thicker cordage initially, but in order to really become proficient with them, you'll need to practice tying them with actual fishing line.

Up until this point, you've probably practiced with nice, soft, supple rope that's easy to work with. Fishing line is an entirely different beast altogether! When you make a wrap with rope, it pretty much stays where you put it until you move along to the next step in tying the knot. On the other hand, when you do the same thing with fishing line, it seems to have a mind of its own, almost as if doesn't want to be tied into a knot at all! It often has a "spring-like" characteristic to it which can make tying these knots quite difficult if you aren't used to tying knots in fishing line.

Another thing that makes tying knots with fishing line difficult is that it is often clear and it can be very thin. This can pose unique challenges, especially if you don't see well up close, or if you have a hard time using your hands to perform delicate procedures that require very fine motor skills. Sometimes it helps to try orienting yourself so that while you are tying a knot, sunlight or even shadows don't impede your ability to see your line well. You'll have to experiment to discover what works best for you.

Keeping in mind that you'll be tying knots in thin line in many cases, it's crucial that you follow the steps in this book properly. The reason for this is when you are tying a knot with rope, you can easily see the finished knot to determine whether it is tied correctly. On the other hand, when you are tying knots in very thin fishing line, unless you have extremely good eyesight, it will likely be difficult to visually inspect the knot after you have tightened it. You'll have to pay close attention and make sure you perform each step carefully. Then you have to trust that it is tied correctly since you won't be able to see the individual parts of the completed knot very well.

A trick many people use to tame this beast known as fishing line is to get into the habit of pinching the knot between their fingers during certain steps. This may help hold the knot in place while you complete the remaining steps. You'll probably have to practice tying these knots a lot if you really want to master them. It might be a good idea to practice using the same type of fishing line you plan on using to try and catch fish with.

Something else to know about tying fishing knots is that you'll need to lubricate the line before you tighten the knot all the way down. This is done so that while you are tightening a knot, the line will slide along itself without creating excess friction which could produce a weak spot. Believe it or not, most anglers just use a little saliva to lubricate the line before tightening. This might sound gross but it works.

Earlier in this book you were advised not to cut the working ends off near the knot. This rule typically doesn't apply to knots used in angling. The reason most anglers trim the working ends off near the knot is because if they leave them long on a fishing knot, fish may see the line more easily. Additionally, the line might snag on debris like slime or moss that may be floating on the water. It's also possible that the lure might not move through the water like it was designed to if the working ends haven't been trimmed off close to the knot. Just remember, if you tie the correct knot for the type of line you're using, make sure it's tied properly, and lubricate it well to ensure it tightens smoothly, your knot shouldn't slip.

While you are tying fishing knots, please don't make the mistake of using your teeth to cut the line as many anglers do. Most who do have ended up chipping their teeth in the process and more than a few have hooked their lips with their fishing lure while doing this!

Nail clippers or a small pair of scissors work very well for trimming fishing line. Not only will you avoid the risk of chipping your teeth if you use these tools, you'll actually be able to trim the leftover section of your working ends much closer to the knot.

Now that you know this series of knots might be tricky to master, remember to have patience and take your time. As you become more and more familiar with how it feels to actually tie knots in fishing line, you'll develop your own technique for getting the job done. Before you know it, you'll be tying fishing knots like a pro!

Arbor Knot

This is the first in a series of fishing knots that will be discussed in this book. You may have heard this one referred to by its more common name as a "slip knot."

Pros: It's extremely simple to tie.

Cons: One negative characteristic of this knot is when you're tying onto a highly polished spool with a very slick surface. Doing this may make it a little difficult to get the knot to constrict tightly enough to prevent it from just slipping as you start winding your line onto the spool.

How to tie it:

1. With the working end you want to tie onto the reel, make a single turn around the spool as illustrated in figure 35a. Since paracord is being used to illustrate the steps involved in tying this knot, an actual fishing reel isn't used in the photographs.

Figure 35a.

2. Take the working end and tie a simple overhand knot around the standing part of your line as illustrated in figure 35b. When you pull this overhand knot tight, make sure to leave a couple of inches on the working end.

Figure 35b.

3. Tie another overhand knot, but this time just tie it in the working end to act as a stopper knot. This step is illustrated in figure 35c. Make sure this stopper knot is close to the first overhand knot you tied in step 2.

Figure 35c.

4. Pull on the standing part and the arbor knot will slip along the standing part and constrict around the spool. The finished knot should look like the one that you see in figure 35d.

Figure 35d.

Possible Uses:

This knot is often used for attaching fishing line to a reel before winding the desired amount onto the spool.

Palomar Knot

The palomar is regarded by many fishermen as one of their favorite knots.

Pros: This knot works well with a variety of types of fishing line and doesn't tend to slip much. The many types of fishing line available today have different characteristics in terms of their ability to hold a knot without slipping. Anglers all over the world like the palomar knot because it can be used whether they're just using common monofilament or the latest high-tech fishing lines.

Cons: If not tied correctly, it can weaken certain types of fishing line, making your line more likely to break at the knot.

How to tie it:

Please note that the photographs used to illustrate each step needed to tie this knot show the knot being tied with a large, homemade hook and paracord. Since paracord doesn't slide along the other strands of itself while tightening, the photos don't precisely illustrate how actual fishing line will lie as the knot is being tightened. Hopefully, you'll still find these photos helpful for learning how to tie this knot.

1. Thread the working end through the eyelet of your hook or lure.

2. Pass the working end back through the eyelet as illustrated in figure 36a. You will essentially have a bight through the eyelet now.

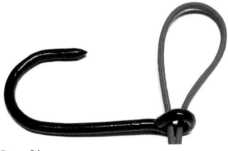

Figure 36a.

3. Cross the bight over both the working end and standing part of your fishing line. This step is illustrated in figure 36b.

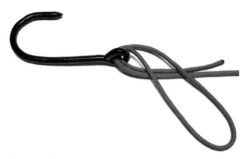

Figure 36b.

4. Taking extra care to not twist the bight, tie a loose over-hand knot with the bight as illustrated in figure 36c. It's important that you don't tighten the overhand knot all the way during this step of the process. Just leave it a bit loose.

Figure 36c.

5. Pass the bight over your hook or lure as illustrated in figure 36d.

Figure 36d.

6. Move the bight towards the standing end, which will be on your fishing reel in this case. Make sure you pass the bight over and around the overhand knot you tied in step 4. This is illustrated in figure 36e.

Figure 36e.

7. Slowly pull on the working end and standing part and the knot will begin to tighten.

8. Before you get the knot all the way tight, you should lubricate it.

9. While carefully holding onto your hook or lure, pull on both the working end and standing part to tighten the knot.

10. You have now completed the palomar knot. The finished knot should look like the one that you see in figure 36f except the working end has not been trimmed in the photo and the knot hasn't been tightened. If you were using this knot to actually tie a hook or lure onto the line, you would want to snip the working end off very close to the knot after you tightened it.

Figure 36f.

Possible Uses:
This knot is used for tying a hook or lure onto a fishing line.

Blood Knot
This knot is commonly used by fly fishermen to join fishing line of various sizes.

Pros: When tied properly, it's a very sleek knot that passes easily through the rod guides on a fishing pole. The nice streamline shape of the blood knot also helps prevent it from accumulating moss and other debris that may be in the water.
Cons: This knot can be very tricky to learn and it isn't a knot that is quickly tied. It requires quite a bit of dexterity as you are tying it as well. You may feel like you need a couple of extra hands to tie this one!

How to tie it:
This is an elegant looking knot but it isn't easily tied with rope because it has too much friction to tighten down properly as described in step 11. In these photographs, blue paracord will be used to represent the thicker line and red paracord will be used to represent the thinner line.

1. Hold the working end of the thicker diameter line in your left hand and the thinner diameter line in your right hand.

Note that for illustration purposes, the blue paracord represents the thicker diameter line and the red paracord represents the thinner diameter line. Also note that although it may not be clear in the illustration, imagine that your hands are holding the lines at the top of the photo, so as stated, the left hand will be holding the blue paracord and your right hand will be holding the red paracord.

2. Cross the two lines over each other so they form an "x" with the thicker line from your left hand lying behind the thinner line in your right hand as illustrated in figure 37a. You'll probably want about five to seven inches of the working ends overlapping each other at this point.

Figure 37a.

3. With the thumb and index finger of your right hand, pinch the "x" where the lines cross to hold the line in place as you complete the next step.

4. Start wrapping the working end of the thinner line around the thicker line. You'll want to wrap in a counterclockwise direction, In other words, pass the thinner line behind the thicker line, over the top and towards you. Complete four to five wraps. When you complete the final wrap, the working end should be pointed down. This is illustrated in figure 37b.

Figure 37b.

5. Bring the working end of the thinner line towards the "x." Pass it through the point where the two lines cross. Make sure the working end of the thinner line is pointed upwards and lying on top of the standing part of itself as illustrated in figure 37c.

Figure 37c.

6. Pinch the knot at this location with your left hand to hold things in place as you continue onto the next step.

7. Now start wrapping the working end of the thicker line in a clockwise direction. In other words, pass the thicker line in front of the thinner line, under and then around towards you. Complete the same number of wraps you made in step 4 to keep the knot symmetrical. When

Figure 37d.

you complete the final wrap, the working end should be pointed up. This is illustrated in figure 37d.

8. Bring the working end of the thicker line towards the working end of the thinner line. Notice that the working end of the thinner line will be treaded through a hole between the two lines and pointed upwards. In this step, you'll want to thread the working end of the thicker line through that same hole but it should go from the top of the hole and be pointing downward. If you've done this correctly, the thinner working end will be pointed up and the thicker working end will be pointed down as illustrated in figure 37e.

Figure 37e.

9. Lubricate the knot and lightly dress it the best you can. It's worth pointing out that the fishing line you're using may seem to have a life of its own when tying this knot. It won't behave like rope and lie neatly as you make the wraps. Just do the best you can to make the wraps and hold everything in place.

10. Gently pull on the standing parts of both lines to take some of the slack out of the knot.

11. Quickly pull the standing parts to tighten the knot. Keep in mind that when tying some knots, they look similar when they are loosely dressed to the way they will look after they are tightened. This knot is a different beast altogether! The finished knot looks nothing like the lightly dressed knot appearing in step 9. When you quickly pull on the standing parts in this step, the wraps tighten in unison and transform as if by magic. It may take several attempts before you get one that looks correct. If you don't perform all the steps correctly when tying this knot, the wraps won't align properly during this step.

12. Trim the working ends off as close to the knot as you can and you have tied a blood knot. The finished knot should look like the one you see in figure 37f.

Figure 37f.

Possible Uses:
This knot can be used to make tapered leaders so your fly fishing line can roll out and gently settle on the water without making a splash that might spook fish.

Surgeon's Knot
This is another useful fishing knot. It's primarily used for joining two lengths of line. When tying the surgeon's knot, the lines should be fairly close in diameter. The lines can have slightly differing diameters, but if they are drastically different you may want to consider using a knot that is better suited for this purpose, such as the blood knot.

Pros: This is a very strong knot that isn't generally believed to weaken the line much. It's also extremely simple to tie.
Cons: This knot can't be easily tied in the middle of your line, therefore it isn't a good choice for tying on a fairly long extension of line onto the line that is already on your reel. It's also one that results in a knot with a slightly larger overall diameter than a blood knot that could be tied with the same two pieces of line.

How to tie it:
Unlike the photographs used to illustrate how to tie the blood knot, in these photographs the red paracord is used to represent the longer main fishing line that is connected

to your reel and blue paracord is used to represent the shorter section of leader or tippet that is being tied onto the end of the main line.

1. First lay the main fishing line and section you are tying on parallel to each other. You'll want to have the working ends overlapping each other by several inches and they should be pointing in opposite directions as illustrated in figure 38a.

Figure 38a.

2. Form the overlapped sections into an overhand loop as illustrated in figure 38b.

Figure 38b.

3. Pass the working ends of both lines through the loop to create a simple overhand knot as illustrated in figure 38c.

Figure 38c.

4. Repeat step 3 as illustrated in figure 38d.

Figure 38d.

5. Lubricate the knot and pull it tight.

6. To complete the surgeon's knot, simply trim the working ends off as close to the knot as possible. The finished knot should look like the one you see in figure 38e but the working ends haven't been trimmed off in the photo. Of course, if you are planning on using this knot for fishing, you'll want to trim these working ends closely to the knot.

Figure 38e.

Possible Uses:

1. The surgeon's knot is often used for tying a leader onto the end of your fishing line.

2. It can also be used to tie a tippet to the end of your fly fishing leader. If you're not familiar with this angling term, a "tippet" is a very lightweight section of monofilament line that is tied onto the end of your leader. The goal is to fool the fish into thinking that the artificial fly at the end of your line is the real deal. By tying a thin tippet to the end of your leader, it makes it possible to cast a fly line so that it gently settles onto the water without making an unnatural splash.

Useful Knot-Tying Resources

While the author has tried to provide thorough written instructions, along with corresponding photographs in this book, you may still find yourself struggling to learn how to tie certain knots. With this in mind, there are plenty of helpful resources available to you on the Internet.

Watching YouTube videos can be extremely helpful but keep in mind that, as mentioned previously in this book, there are often multiple ways of tying various knots. You may watch one video to learn how to tie a particular knot only to find that another video provides slightly different instructions or methods.

There are also some websites that specialize in providing step-by-step instructions to help you learn how to tie the knots described in this book. Two websites the author recommends are animatedknots.com and netknots.com. The reason she likes these websites is that, in addition to providing written instructions, they provide very helpful animations she finds particularly useful when learning how to tie a new knot.

Summary

Now that you understand some of what you need to know about rope and some multi-purpose knots that a prepper might choose to use, the rest is up to you. Always remember that prepping is all about becoming as prepared as you possibly can. Of course, this includes stockpiling supplies but don't forget that it's just as important to fill your mind with useful information you can draw upon in any type of crisis that you might find yourself faced with.

While knowledge is important, when you practice putting the knowledge that you have to use, you develop skills. It's the opinion of this author that becoming proficient with survival skills is as important, and maybe even more important, than simply having a large stockpile of supplies.

You are encouraged to take what you have learned in this book and put it to use in your day to day lives. Develop the skills necessary to tie these knots as effortlessly as you tie your shoelaces every morning. You'll undoubtedly find many uses for the knots you learn how to tie in this book, even if you never have to use them in a survival situation. With that in mind, if you do ever have to use your supplies and skills to endure the aftermath of a major emergency, you'll be really glad that you read this book and took the time to become a master at tying prepper knots!

Sign Up for Free Weekly Updates from Preppers Illustrated

I sincerely hope you found the information in this book helpful! If you did, you might be interested in knowing that I provide a free service where I'll send you prepping tips in the form of an email. I HIGHLY suggest you take a brief moment and sign up now! When you do, you'll get a **FREE** copy of my eBook titled, *165 Items That Preppers Might Forget to Store with Their Emergency Supplies.*

Don't worry; I won't start spamming your inbox with hundreds of useless emails. I will, however, send you free updates from *Preppers Illustrated* right to your inbox that will hopefully help you to become a better prepper.

It takes less than thirty seconds to sign up and you don't even have to give me your name. All you need to do is enter your email address on a simple form after going to preppersillustrated.com/sign-up. If I don't live up to your expectations, you can easily unsubscribe by clicking on the link labeled "unsubscribe" found at the bottom of every email I send you.

Please Follow Me on Social Media!

I would also really appreciate it if you would follow me on my social media pages. Doing so will mean that you'll be able to receive even more helpful emergency preparedness tips. Besides, being social is fun!

Pinterest: pinterest.com/theppermag
Twitter: twitter.com/ThePrepperMag
Facebook: facebook.com/PreppersIllustrated
YouTube: bit.ly/youtube-preppers-illustrated

Don't Be a Stranger!

I love connecting and interacting with other likeminded people, especially preppers! As mentioned above, please feel free to connect with me on social media. That's a great way of sharing ideas. With this being said, I also welcome emails from anyone who has questions or ideas about prepping. Feel free to send me an email at pattyhahne@preppersillustrated.com.